Mastering Your Finances

A Comprehensive Guide to Finances

Written by
Michaela McGee

So You Can Write PublicationsTM
P.O. Box 80736
Milwaukee, WI 53208
Phone: (920)-821-3006

Library of Congress Cataloging-in-Publication Data

Published by So You Can Write Publications, LLC

www.sycwp.com
home4writers@sycwp.com

ISBN: 979-8-9899762-0-1

SO YOU CAN WRITE
PUBLICATIONS®

TABLE OF CONTENTS

DEDICATION

In the quiet corners of our lives, there exists a force that shapes us, molds us, and propels us forward on our journey. For me, that driving force has always been my dad. From the very beginning, he instilled in me a sense of wonder and possibility, igniting a fire within my heart to live the life I imagined for myself. My dad's compassionate nature and genuine kindness have left a permanent mark in my heart.

From a young age, my dad has been my biggest supporter, constantly reminding me that I am capable of achieving greatness. He has nurtured my aspirations, urging me to dream big and never settle for anything less than the desires of my heart. It is through his unwavering belief in me that I found the strength to pursue my goals. He would always encourage me to follow the desires of my heart.

QUESTIONNAIRE

What do you know about financial literacy?

_____

_____

_____

What financial tools do you have in place
when you get "STUCK"?

_____

_____

_____

What are your greatest and least greatest
financial accomplishments?

_____

_____

_____

What are your financial strengths and weaknesses?

_____

_____

_____

_____

What finance strategies are important to you?

_____

_____

_____

Are you where you thought you would be financially?

_____

_____

_____

What motivates you?

_____

_____

_____

What type of financial goals would you like to achieve?

_____

_____

_____

Are you ready to learn and collect tools to live in financial freedom?

_____

_____

_____

_____

Chapter 1

Building a Strong Financial Foundation

Understanding the Importance of Financial Literacy

In today's world, where money plays such a significant role in our lives, it is crucial to have a solid understanding of financial matters. Financial literacy is the knowledge and skills required to make informed decisions about money management. It goes beyond simply knowing how to balance a checkbook or pay bills on time; it encompasses a wide range of essential concepts such as budgeting, saving, investing, and understanding credit.

Why is financial literacy so important? It empowers individuals to take control of their finances. By understanding how money works, individuals can make informed decisions about their income, expenses, and investments. They can create budgets that align with their personal financial goals, differentiate between needs and wants, and plan for the future. Financially literate individuals are less likely to make impulsive purchases.

Next, financial literacy is essential for economic stability and growth. When individuals have a solid understanding of financial matters, they are more likely to contribute positively to the economy. They are more likely to save and invest their money, which leads to capital formation and economic growth. On the other hand, individuals who lack financial literacy may struggle with managing debt, making sound investments, and planning for retirement. This can lead to financial instability and can have a negative impact not only on the individual but also on the economy as a whole.

Additionally, financial literacy is crucial for building wealth and achieving financial goals. By understanding the concepts of saving, investing, and budgeting, individuals can make their money work for them. They can identify opportunities for growth and make smart investment decisions that can yield significant returns over time. Financially literate individuals are also more likely to set and achieve their financial goals since they have a clear understanding of what it takes to reach them.

Moreover, financial literacy is an important life skill that should be taught in the education curriculum. Financial decisions are a part of everyday life, and having a strong foundation in financial literacy can set individuals on the path to long-term financial success. By teaching children the basics of money management, such as budgeting and saving, we can instill good financial habits that will benefit them throughout their lives.

Unfortunately, despite the importance of financial literacy, studies have shown that a significant portion of the population lacks the necessary knowledge and skills in this area. This highlights the need for educational efforts to improve financial literacy rates. Educational institutions, financial institutions,and government agencies can play a significant role in promoting financial literacy by introducing financial literacy programs and resources. These programs can provide individuals with the information and tools they need to make informed financial decisions.

Financial literacy programs can cover a wide range of financial topics, including budgeting, saving, investing, and managing debt. They can also teach individuals about important financial concepts such as compound interest, inflation, and diversification. By providing individuals with this knowledge, they can make better financial decisions and improve their overall financial well-being.

In addition to educational programs, other resources such as online tools and apps can also be beneficial in improving financial literacy. These resources can provide individuals with interactive experiences and simulations, making it easier for them to understand complex financial concepts. Furthermore, they can also help individuals track their spending, set financial goals, and manage their budget effectively.

Ultimately, improving financial literacy is an ongoing process that requires individuals to take responsibility for their financial well-being. It requires individuals to educate themselves, seek out resources, and make an effort to improve their financial knowledge and skills. By doing so, individuals can build a strong financial foundation and set themselves up for long-term financial success.

Financial literacy is a crucial skill that everyone should strive to master. It empowers individuals to take control of their finances, contributes to economic stability and growth, and helps individuals build wealth and achieve their financial goals. It is an essential life skill that should be taught from an early age and can be supported through educational programs and resources. By improving financial literacy rates, we can create a society where individuals have the knowledge and skills to make informed financial decisions and create a prosperous future for themselves.

Creating a Budget Strategy

These strategies will help you create a solid budgeting strategy that will put you on the path to financial success. Financial management and budgeting is a reflection on your personal relationship and understanding of expenses.

1. Define your financial goals: Before you can create a budget, it's important to know what you are working towards. Set clear financial goals for yourself, whether it is saving for a down payment on a house, paying off debt, or saving for retirement. Having specific goals will give you a clear direction and purpose for your budget.

2. Track your income and expenses: Start by writing down all of your sources of income, including your salary, side hustles, and any other streams of money that comes into your household. Then, track your expenses for at least three months to get an accurate picture of where your money is going. This includes everything from bills and groceries to entertainment and dining out. This will help you identify areas where you can cut back and allocate more funds towards your desired financial goals.

3. Categorize your expenses: Once you have a clear understanding of your expenses, categorize them into fixed and variable expenses. Fixed expenses are those that stay consistent from month to month, such as rent or mortgage payments, car payments, and insurance premiums. Variable expenses are those that fluctuate, such as groceries, dining out, and entertainment. This segmentation will help you identify where

you have the most flexibility to cut back.

4. Determine your essential and non-essential expenses: Take a closer look at your variable expenses and categorize them as essential or non-essential. Essential expenses are those that are necessary for basic living, such as groceries, utilities, and transportation. Non-essential expenses are those that are optional and can be eliminated or reduced if necessary, such as eating out or cable subscriptions. By identifying your non-essential expenses, you can find areas to cut back and allocate more funds towards your financial goals.

5. Create a realistic budget: Based on your income and expenses, create a budget that aligns with your financial goals. Start by allocating funds towards your essential expenses, making sure to prioritize items such as housing, food, and transportation. Then, allocate funds towards your financial goals, whether it's paying off debt or saving for retirement. Finally, allocate funds towards your non-essential expenses, making sure to limit spending in these areas to what you can afford.

6. Monitor and adjust your budget: Once you've created your budget, it's important to monitor your progress and make adjustments as needed. Keep track of your expenses on a regular basis and compare them to your budgeted amounts. This will help you identify any areas where you may be overspending or where you can make further cuts. If necessary, adjust your budget as needed to ensure that you're staying on track towards your financial goals.

7. Be flexible and forgiving: Budgeting is a continuous process, and it's important to be flexible and forgiving with

yourself. Unexpected expenses or changes in income may require adjustments to your budget. Don't beat yourself up if you overspend or deviate from your budget occasionally. Instead, learn from your mistakes and use them as an opportunity to refine your budgeting strategy.

8. Know your budget: You must know how much cashflow you have so you know how much you can spend. Your cash flow is the available funds after all monthly expenses have been paid. (Know what you have, so you know what you can spend)

Use tools to help you make effective choices with your funds.

If you are not able to pay cash money for something, then you cannot afford it. Do not purchase it.

Set annual goals on what you save monthly, quarterly, or annually.

Build a financial action plan quarterly or bi-yearly and execute (set a goal and stick to it).

Pay your debt in full before you make big purchases.

Know where you spend your money. Take the last three months of your bank statements and review to determine where you spend your money then create a financial action plan.

Once you determine where you spend your money you can create a realistic financial action plan. If your findings are $500 in food and entertainment, if you adjust this amount, you will have $500 to plan towards financial freedom.

Do not spend money in your hometown, spend money when you travel.

Plan where your earnings will go, if you bring home 7K and 4K covers all monthly expenses, the remaining 3K goes toward what?

Teach yourself to not spend carelessly by managing what you own and live a life with less. Thank me someday once you master this one. This is one of my favorites.

Invest in your future, be certain to place funds aside in an investment account where your money grows.

Plan an annual shopping budget and stick to it, spending money all year round will not lead to financial freedom.

By following these budgeting strategies, you can create a strong financial foundation and take control of your finances. Remember, budgeting is a tool that empowers you to make informed financial decisions and work towards your financial goals. Stay disciplined and focused, and you will build a strong financial future.

Developing Good
Saving Habits

Saving money is an essential aspect of building a strong financial foundation. It allows you to have a cushion for unexpected emergencies, achieve financial goals, and provide for a comfortable future. However, developing good saving habits can be challenging in today's consumer-driven society. Here are some tips to help you develop a saving mindset and build a healthy savings habit:

1. Set achievable savings goals: Start by setting specific and achievable savings goals. Whether it is saving for a vacation, a down payment on a house, or an emergency fund, having a clear goal will motivate you to save regularly. Break down your larger goal into smaller, manageable chunks, and create a timeline for achieving each milestone.

2. Create a budget: A budget is a tool that helps you track your income and expenses, and it is essential for saving money effectively. Start by analyzing your spending habits and identifying areas where you can cut back. Create a budget that includes saving as a priority, and allocate a portion of your income towards your savings goals. Stick to this budget and adjust it as needed to ensure you are on track with your savings goals.

3. Automate your savings: Take advantage of automation to make saving money easier. Set up automatic transfers from your checking account to your investment portfolio account on a regular basis. This way, you will not have to manually transfer the money, and eliminate your temptation to spend

it. Treat your investment portfolio as a fixed expense that you prioritize every month.

4. Cut back on unnecessary expenses: Take a closer look at your spending habits and identify areas where you can cut back. This can include eating out less often, reducing entertainment expenses, or finding cheaper alternatives for certain products or services. Remember, every penny you save adds up, and cutting back on unnecessary expenses can free up more money for your savings.

5. Pay yourself first: Make saving a priority by paying yourself first. Before paying your bills or spending money on nonessential items, allocate a portion of your income to your savings. This ensures that you prioritize saving and gradually build up your savings over time.

6. Start an emergency fund: An emergency fund is an essential component of financial security. Aim to save at least three to six months' worth of living expenses in case of emergencies such as job loss, medical expenses, or unexpected car repairs. Having an emergency fund not only provides peace of mind but also prevents you from going into debt when unexpected expenses arise.

7. Find ways to increase your income: Explore opportunities to increase your income by taking on a side gig or finding ways to earn extra money outside of your regular job. Use this income to boost your savings and accelerate your progress towards your goals.

8. Stay motivated and celebrate milestones: Saving money re-

quires discipline and perseverance, so it is crucial to stay motivated along the way. Celebrate your savings milestones and reward yourself for reaching your goals, whether it is with a small treat or a meaningful experience. This positive reinforcement will keep you motivated and encourage you to continue saving.

Remember, developing good saving habits takes time and practice. Start small, be consistent, and adjust your habits as needed. With dedication and perseverance, you can build a healthy savings habit that will lead to financial security and freedom.

Chapter 2

Managing Debt Effectively

Different Types of Debts: Credit Cards, Student Loans, Mortgages

The Importance of Credit and Maintaining a Good Credit Score.

Credit plays a crucial role in our financial lives, and understanding how it works is essential for managing debt effectively and building a strong financial foundation. Credit allows us to make purchases and borrow money for various purposes such as buying a car, getting a mortgage, or funding education expenses.

However, to access credit, you need a good credit score. Here is why credit is important and how you can maintain a good credit score:

1. Access to better borrowing options: Having a good credit score opens doors to better borrowing options. Lenders use your credit score to assess your creditworthiness and determine if they should lend you money. A good credit score demonstrates that you are responsible with credit and more likely to repay your debts on time. This can result in lower interest rates, higher credit limits, and better terms when accessing credit products such as loans and credit cards.

2. Lower interest rates: Your credit score influences the interest rates you are offered on borrowed funds. A good credit score is associated with lower interest rates, which can save you significant amounts of money over time. With a lower interest rate, your monthly payments will be more manageable, and you will pay less in interest charges throughout the life of the loan.

3. Access to housing and rental opportunities: A good credit score is not only important for borrowing money but also for accessing housing and rental opportunities. Landlords and property managers often review your credit history to assess your financial responsibility. A good credit score can increase your chances of being approved for a rental property or securing a mortgage to purchase a home.

4. Employment opportunities: Some employers perform credit checks as part of their pre-employment screening process. While your credit score does not determine your job qualifications, some employers may consider it as an indicator of financial responsibility and trustworthiness. Maintaining a good credit score can be beneficial for your job prospects.

5. Insurance rates: Insurers may use your credit score to determine the rates you are offered for auto, home, or other types of insurance. A good credit score can result in lower insurance premiums, saving you money on your coverage.

To maintain a good credit score and reap these benefits, follow these tips:

1. Pay your bills on time: Payment history is the most crucial factor in determining your credit score. Make sure to pay your bills, including credit cards, loans, and utilities, on time. Late payments can negatively impact your credit score and remain on your credit report for up to seven years.

2. Keep your credit utilization low: Credit utilization is the percentage of your available credit that you are using. It is recommended to keep your credit utilization below 30% to

maintain a good credit score. By keeping your balances low, you demonstrate responsible credit management and show lenders that you can handle credit responsibly.

3. Monitor your credit report regularly: Your credit report provides a detailed history of your credit activity, including open accounts, payment history, and any negative information. Regularly reviewing your credit report allows you to identify errors, fraudulent activities, or signs of identity theft. You can obtain a free copy of your credit report from each of the three major credit bureaus once a year.

4. Diversify your credit mix: Lenders like to see a diverse credit mix, including a combination of credit cards, loans, and mortgages. Having a mix of credit accounts shows your ability to manage different types of credit responsibly.

5. Avoid unnecessary credit applications: Every time you apply for new credit, it generates a hard inquiry on your credit report. Multiple hard inquiries can lower your credit score temporarily. Only apply for credit when necessary and be mindful of the impact on your credit score.

Credit is an essential tool in managing debt and building a strong financial foundation. Maintaining a good credit score allows you to access better borrowing options, save money on interest rates, and open doors to various opportunities. By following these tips and practicing responsible credit habits, you can maintain a good credit score and reap the benefits that come with it.

Mastering financial literacy is crucial for managing debt effectively and building a strong financial foundation. By understanding the importance of financial literacy, individuals can take control of their finances, contribute to economic stability, and achieve their financial goals. Strategies for debt management and repayment, as well as cultivating good saving habits and maintaining a good credit score, play essential roles in this process. With the right knowledge, skills, and strategies, individuals can navigate the complex world of finances, make informed decisions, and create a secure and prosperous financial future.

Strategies for Debt Management and Repayment

In today's fast-paced and consumer-driven society, it is no surprise that many individuals find themselves burdened with debt. From student loans to credit card debt, the pressure to "keep up with the Joneses" can often lead to financial strain and anxiety. However, it is important to remember that debt is not the end of the world. With the right strategies and a positive mindset, anyone can master the art of managing debt effectively and embark on a journey towards financial freedom.

One of the first steps towards successful debt management is to create a realistic budget. This will help to determine how much money can be allocated towards debt repayment each month. It is essential to prioritize debt payments and make them a non-negotiable part of the budget. By setting aside a specific amount each month, individuals can systematically chip away at their debt and avoid falling into the trap of only making minimum payments.

In addition to budgeting, it is crucial to take a proactive approach to debt management. This means actively seeking out ways to reduce interest rates and negotiate with creditors. Consider contacting credit card companies to explore options for lowering interest rates or consolidating debt into a personal loan with a lower interest rate. Taking advantage of balance transfer offers can also be a useful tool for consolidating debt and reducing interest payments.

Another effective strategy for managing debt is to prioritize which debts to focus on first. Many financial experts recommend the "snowball method", which involves paying off the smallest debts first while continuing to make minimum payments on larger debts. As each debt is paid off, the individual gains momentum and motivation to tackle the next debt, creating a snowball effect. Alternatively, some individuals may prefer the "avalanche method", which involves prioritizing debts based on interest rates. By paying off debts with the highest interest rates first, individuals can save money in the long run.

It is important to remember that managing debt effectively also requires a mindset shift. Instead of dwelling on past mistakes or succumbing to feelings of shame and guilt, individuals should approach debt repayment with a positive and proactive attitude. Celebrate small wins along the way, such as paying off a credit card or reducing interest rates. By focusing on progress rather than the amount of debt remaining, individuals can stay motivated and committed to their financial goals.

In addition to these strategies, it can be helpful to seek professional advice and guidance when it comes to managing debt. Financial advisors and credit counselors can provide valuable insights and personalized strategies for debt repayment based on individual circumstances. They can also assist in creating a realistic budget and developing a long-term financial plan to prevent future debt.

Furthermore, it is important to stay educated and informed about personal finance. Financial literacy is crucial for understanding concepts such as interest rates, credit scores, and debt-to-income ratios. Take advantage of resources such as books, online articles, and financial podcasts to increase knowledge and stay up to date on the latest trends in personal finance. The more knowledgeable individuals are, the better equipped they will be to make informed decisions and take control of their financial lives.

Lastly, it is important to practice patience and resilience on the journey to debt freedom. Managing debt effectively requires time and consistency. It is unlikely that debts will magically disappear overnight, but with continued effort and determination, individuals can make significant strides towards a debt-free future. Remember to be kind to oneself throughout the process, understanding that setbacks and challenges are a natural part of the journey.

Mastering financial literacy and managing debt effectively is possible for anyone. By creating a realistic budget, being proactive in seeking out options for reducing interest rates, and prioritizing debt repayment, individuals can take control of their financial situations. A positive mindset, combined with professional advice and education, will contribute to the ability to stay motivated and maintain long-term financial success. With patience and resilience, debt can be conquered, leading to a brighter and more secure financial future.

How to Improve Your Credit Score

In today's financial landscape, managing debt has become an essential skill for individuals seeking long-term financial stability. One crucial aspect of this endeavor is understanding how to improve your credit score. While debt may sometimes feel overwhelming, taking control of your financial situation and adopting a positive mindset can lead to significant improvements in your creditworthiness. This essay aims to explore practical strategies for managing debt effectively and enhancing your credit score, all with an optimistic outlook towards building a brighter future.

1. Developing a Positive Mindset: Managing debt effectively begins with cultivating a positive mindset. Rather than viewing debt as a burden, consider it an opportunity for growth and improvement. By embracing a positive attitude and acknowledging that your current financial situation is temporary, you can start making proactive changes to achieve your desired credit score.

2. Create a Solid Budget: The cornerstone of effective debt management is creating a robust budget that allows you to live within your means while gradually paying down your debts. Start by identifying all your sources of income and categorizing your expenses, including fixed costs like rent or mortgage payments, utilities, and insurance. Then, allocate a portion of your income towards repaying debts and saving for emergencies. Sticking to a budget will help you regain

control over your finances and establish a strong foundation for improving your credit score.

3. Prioritize Debt Repayment: Debt repayment should be a top priority to effectively manage your debts and improve your credit score. Begin by identifying your highest interest debts and allocating additional funds to pay them off as quickly as possible. Adopting a strategy such as the debt avalanche method, wherein you pay off debts with the highest interest rates first, can save you money on interest payments in the long run.

4. Communication and Negotiation: If you find yourself struggling to meet your debt obligations, do not hesitate to reach out to your creditors. Many lenders offer options for debt restructuring, which can provide temporary relief from high payments. By communicating openly and honestly about your financial situation, you may be able to negotiate more favorable terms such as reduced interest rates or extended repayment periods. This proactive approach demonstrates your commitment to fulfilling your obligations and can positively impact your credit score.

5. Building and Improving Credit: Apart from managing debts, actively working towards improving your credit score is crucial for long-term financial success. A good credit score opens doors to favorable interest rates on loans, credit card approvals, and even rental applications. Here are some strategies to improve your credit score effectively:

6. Pay Your Bills on Time: Consistently paying your bills on time is one of the simplest and most effective ways to estab-

lish a positive credit history. Even a single late payment can have a negative impact on your credit score. Set up automatic bill payments or use reminders to ensure you never miss a due date. Over time, this responsible payment behavior will reflect positively on your credit report.

7. Utilize Credit Wisely: While it may be tempting to max out available credit, responsible credit utilization is key to improving your credit score. Aim to keep your credit utilization ratio below 30%, meaning you should only utilize 30% or less of your available credit. Paying down credit card balances and avoiding excessive debt can positively impact your creditworthiness, demonstrating that you can manage credit responsibly.

8. Monitor your Credit Report: Regularly checking your credit report will help you identify any errors or inaccuracies that could be negatively affecting your credit score. If you find any discrepancies, promptly dispute them with the credit bureaus to ensure your report accurately reflects your credit history. Monitoring your credit report also allows you to track your progress and celebrate milestones as your credit score improves.

Effectively managing debt and improving your credit score requires a combination of proactive financial strategies and a positive mindset. By creating a solid budget, prioritizing debt repayment, and maintaining open communication with creditors, you can take control of your financial situation. Similarly, paying your bills on time, utilizing credit responsibly, and monitoring your credit report are critical steps towards improving your creditworthiness. Embracing these strategies, along with an optimistic outlook towards building a brighter financial future, will empower you to achieve your goals, secure favorable interest rates, and unlock a world of possibilities. Remember, by taking control of your debt and credit, you have the potential to build a strong foundation for a more prosperous and fulfilling life.

Chapter 3

Investing for the Future

Introduction to Investing:
Stocks, Bonds, Mutual Funds

When it comes to securing a stable and prosperous financial future, investing is an essential component. Investing allows individuals to grow their wealth and achieve long-term financial goals. However, for those new to the world of investing, the options and strategies can be overwhelming. In this comprehensive guide, we will introduce the basics of investing, including stocks, bonds, and mutual funds, providing a solid foundation for individuals to begin their investment journey.

One of the most common forms of investment is stocks. A stock represents a share in the ownership of a company. When you buy stocks, you become a partial owner of the company and have the potential to benefit from its success. Stocks offer the opportunity for capital appreciation, dividend income, and the ability to vote on important corporate decisions. It is important to conduct thorough research and analysis before investing in individual stocks, as the value of a stock can be influenced by a variety of factors, including company performance, market conditions, and industry trends.

For those looking for a more diversified approach to investing, bonds can be an attractive option. Bonds are debt securities issued by governments, municipalities, and corporations. When you invest in bonds, you are essentially lending money to the issuer in exchange for regular interest payments and the return of the principal amount at maturity. Bonds are considered lower risk compared to stocks, as they provide a fixed income stream and are generally less volatile. However, it is important to assess the creditworthiness of the bond issuer before investing, as the risk of default can vary among different entities.

Mutual funds are another popular investment vehicle that offers diversification and professional management. A mutual fund pools money from multiple investors to invest in a diversified portfolio of stocks, bonds, or both. By investing in a mutual fund, individuals can gain exposure to a wide range of securities, even with a small investment amount. Mutual funds are typically managed by professional fund managers who make investment decisions on behalf of the investors. This alleviates the need for individual stock selection and allows investors to benefit from the expertise of the fund manager.

When it comes to investing, it is crucial to understand the concept of risk and return. Generally, investments with higher potential returns come with higher levels of risk. Stocks, for example, have the potential for substantial gains but also carry the risk of significant losses. On the other hand, bonds, especially those issued by reputable entities, offer lower returns but are considered safer investments. Mutual funds fall somewhere in between, depending on the specific assets and strategies employed by the fund.

Diversification is another important principle in investing. It involves spreading investments across different asset classes, sectors, and regions to reduce the risk of exposure to a single security or market. Diversification can help protect against losses and improve the potential for long-term returns.

By investing in a mix of stocks, bonds, and other assets, individuals can create a well-diversified portfolio that can better withstand market fluctuations.

Investing is not a one-time activity. It requires regular monitoring and adjustment to ensure that your investment portfolio stays aligned with your financial goals and risk tolerance. Market conditions, economic factors, and personal circumstances can all impact the performance of investments. Therefore, it is important to regularly review your portfolio, reassess your investment objectives, and make necessary adjustments if needed.

To effectively invest for the future, it is crucial to have a long-term perspective. Investing is not a get-rich-quick scheme, but rather a gradual process of building wealth over time. It is normal for investments to experience fluctuations and short-term volatility. However, by staying focused on your long-term goals and maintaining a disciplined approach, you can ride out market ups and downs and benefit from the power of compounding over time.

Finally, it is recommended to seek professional advice when it comes to investing. Financial advisors can provide personalized guidance based on your individual financial situation, goals, and risk tolerance. They can help you develop an investment strategy, select suitable investments, and navigate through market uncertainties. Additionally, they can provide ongoing support and education, ensuring that you stay on track towards your long-term financial objectives.

Investing is a crucial component of building a secure and prosperous financial future. By understanding the basics of investing and familiarizing yourself with various investment options such as stocks, bonds, and mutual funds, you can lay a solid foundation for your investment journey. Remember to consider risk and return, diversify your portfolio, regularly review and adjust investments, maintain a long-term perspective, and seek professional advice when needed. With patience, discipline, and a commitment to continued learning, you can set yourself up for success in investing for the future.

Diversification and Risk Management

Financial literacy is a vital skill for anyone looking to navigate the complexities of the financial world effectively. Understanding the concepts of diversification and risk management is crucial for achieving long-term financial goals and securing a stable financial future. In this comprehensive guide, we will explore the importance of diversification and risk management, providing valuable insights and strategies for mastering these essential financial skills.

Diversification involves spreading your investments across different asset classes, sectors, and geographic regions to reduce the risk of exposure to a single investment. The old saying, "Don't put all your eggs in one basket," perfectly captures the essence of diversification. By investing in a variety of assets, such as stocks, bonds, real estate, and commodities, you can reduce the impact of a single investment's poor performance on your overall portfolio.

Diversification helps to mitigate risk by reducing the likelihood of losses in your investments. If one asset class or sector is underperforming, the gains from other investments can help offset the losses. This can provide a smoother investment journey, reducing the impact of market volatility and improving the chances of achieving long-term financial goals.

However, diversification does not guarantee profits or protect against all losses. It is crucial to carefully select and allocate your investments based on your risk tolerance, financial goals, and time horizon. The key is to strike the right balance between risk and potential return by diversifying your investments across different asset classes that align with your investment objectives.

In addition to diversification, effective risk management is essential in maintaining a healthy investment portfolio. Risk management involves identifying and assessing potential risks and implementing strategies to mitigate them. Each investment carries its own level of risk, and it is important to understand the risks associated with each investment option.

One strategy for risk management is setting clear investment goals and establishing a time horizon for each investment. Short-term investments may have different risk profiles compared to long-term investments. By aligning your investment choices with your time horizon, you can better manage risk and avoid making impulsive investment decisions based on short-term market fluctuations.

Another risk management strategy is regularly reviewing and rebalancing your portfolio. As investment values change, your portfolio's asset allocation can drift from your original plan. Rebalancing involves adjusting your holdings to maintain the desired portfolio mix. This ensures that you stay on track with your investment objectives and reduces the risk of being overly exposed to a particular asset class or sector.

Furthermore, staying informed and continuously educating yourself about the financial markets and economic trends is crucial for effective risk management. Keep up-to-date with market news, economic indicators, and any significant events that may impact your investments. By being informed, you can make well-informed decisions and adjust your portfolio as necessary.

Seeking professional advice is also a valuable risk management strategy. Financial advisors can provide personalized guidance based on your individual financial situation, risk tolerance, and investment goals. They can help you develop a comprehensive financial plan and investment strategy that aligns with your objectives. Regularly consulting with a financial advisor can ensure that you stay on track and make informed decisions, especially during turbulent market periods.

Mastering financial literacy involves understanding the importance of diversification and risk management. Diversification helps spread investments across various assets, sectors, and regions, reducing the impact of poor performance in individual investments. Risk management involves identifying and assessing potential risks and implementing strategies to mitigate them. By setting clear investment goals, regularly reviewing and rebalancing your portfolio, staying informed, and seeking professional advice, you can effectively manage risks and increase your chances of achieving long-term financial success. Remember, proper diversification and risk management are essential tools on the path to mastering financial literacy and securing a stable financial future.

Retirement Planning and Investment Strategies

Retirement planning is a critical aspect of financial literacy that often gets overlooked. It is essential to plan and prepare for retirement to ensure a comfortable and financially secure future. In this comprehensive guide, we will discuss the importance of retirement planning and explore various investment strategies that can help you achieve your retirement goals.

Retirement planning starts with setting clear financial goals for your retirement. Determine how much income you will need during retirement to maintain your desired lifestyle. Consider factors such as housing expenses, healthcare costs, travel, and any other expenses that may arise. By estimating your retirement income needs, you can develop a savings plan to help you reach your goals.

One popular and effective retirement savings option is an employer-sponsored retirement plan, such as a 401(k) or 403(b) plan. These plans allow you to contribute a portion of your pre-tax earnings, and some employers even match your contributions up to a certain percentage. Take advantage of employer matching contributions, as it is essentially free money that can significantly boost your retirement savings.

Individual retirement accounts (IRAs) are another valuable tool for retirement planning. Traditional IRAs allow you to contribute pre-tax dollars, which may provide a tax deduction in the year of contribution. This means that the amount you contribute to a traditional IRA can be deducted from your taxable income, potentially reducing your overall tax liability for the year. Additionally, any earnings within the IRA grow on a tax-deferred basis, meaning you won't owe taxes on the growth until you withdraw the funds in retirement. This can allow your investments to compound over time, potentially leading to significant growth.

Another benefit of traditional IRAs is that they offer flexibility in terms of investment options. With a traditional IRA, you can choose from a wide range of investment vehicles, including stocks, bonds, mutual funds, and even real estate. This gives you the opportunity to tailor your investment strategy to your risk tolerance and financial goals.

Furthermore, traditional IRAs also offer a level of control and ownership over your retirement savings. Unlike employer-sponsored retirement plans like 401(k)s, IRAs are individual accounts that you have complete control over. This means that you can choose when to contribute, how much to contribute, and how to invest those contributions. This flexibility can be particularly valuable if you change jobs or if you want to have more control over your retirement savings.

Traditional IRAs provide tax advantages, investment flexibility, and control over your retirement savings , making them a valuable tool for retirement planning. By contributing pre-tax dollars, you can potentially lower your taxable income and reduce your overall tax liability. The tax-deferred growth of earnings within the IRA allows your investments to grow over time without incurring taxes until you withdraw the funds in retirement.

Additionally, traditional IRAs offer a wide range of investment options, allowing you to tailor your investment strategy according to your risk tolerance and financial goals. This flexibility can help you optimize your investment returns and potentially increase your retirement savings.

Moreover, traditional IRAs give you complete control and ownership over your retirement savings. Unlike employer-sponsored plans, you have the freedom to contribute when and how much you want, as well as the ability to choose from various investment vehicles. This control allows you to have a more personalized approach to saving for retirement and gives you the ability to make adjustments as needed.

Traditional IRAs offer tax advantages, investment flexibility, and control over your retirement savings, making them a valuable tool for anyone planning for retirement. Consider opening a traditional IRA as part of your overall retirement strategy and consult with a financial advisor to determine the best approach for your individual needs and circumstances.

Chapter 4

Building Long-Term Wealth

Real Estate Investment and Property Ownership

Building Long-Term Wealth with Real Estate Investment and Property Ownership

For those seeking to build wealth over the long-term, real estate investment and property ownership can be an excellent strategy. Real estate has been a reliable and profitable investment option for centuries, and it continues to provide opportunities for growth and financial security.

One of the key advantages of investing in real estate is the potential for steady cash flow. When you own a rental property, you can generate income on a consistent basis through rent payments. This income can provide a stable source of cash flow, allowing you to cover expenses and potentially earn a profit.

Moreover, real estate has the potential for appreciation over time. While property values can fluctuate in the short-term, historically, real estate has shown to appreciate in value over the long-term. As the population grows and demand for housing increases, the value of real estate tends to rise. This appreciation can help you build wealth and increase your net worth over time.

Real estate also provides a unique tax advantage. The income generated from rental property can be taxed at a lower rate than other forms of income. Additionally, you can deduct certain expenses related to property ownership, such as property taxes and insurance, from your taxable income. These tax benefits can help you save money and increase your overall return on investment.

Another advantage of real estate investment is the ability to leverage your investment. When purchasing a property, you can finance a large portion of the purchase price through a mortgage. This allows you to control a significant asset with a relatively small upfront investment. By using leverage, you can amplify your returns and potentially increase your wealth at a faster rate.

Real estate also provides diversification to your investment portfolio. By including real estate in your investment mix, you can spread your risk across different asset classes. This can help mitigate the impact of market fluctuations in other investment areas and provide a stable base for your overall portfolio.

Additionally, real estate provides a tangible asset that you can see and touch. Unlike stocks, bonds, or other financial instruments, real estate is a physical asset that you can physically visit and assess. This gives investors a greater sense of control and security, as they can personally monitor the condition and value of their investment.

Moreover, real estate provides the opportunity to generate passive income, particularly through rental properties. Once you have purchased a property, you can hire a property management company to handle the day-to-day operations and maintenance. This allows you to earn income without actively managing the property yourself, giving you more time and freedom to focus on other aspects of your life.

Real estate investment and property ownership also have the potential for long-term wealth and generational wealth. By acquiring property and holding onto it for an extended period of time, you can benefit from the compounding effects of appreciation and rental income. Real estate has proven to be a reliable long-term investment, and by holding onto properties for multiple generations, you can pass down a valuable asset to your children and grandchildren.

In addition to the financial benefits, real estate investment and property ownership can also provide other advantages. For example, owning rental properties can provide a stable source of income during retirement or other periods of life when you may need additional financial support. It can also provide a sense of pride and accomplishment to own and manage properties, and it can serve as a valuable asset that can be used as collateral for other investments or financial opportunities.

Of course, like any investment, there are risks associated with real estate investment and property ownership. Property values can decline, tenants can default on rent payments, and unexpected expenses can arise. However, by conducting thorough research, investing in good locations, and diversifying your investment portfolio, you can mitigate these risks and increase your chances of success.

Real Estate investment and property ownership can be a powerful strategy for building long-term wealth. With the potential for steady cash flow, appreciation, tax advantages, leverage, diversification, passive income, and the ability to generate generational wealth, real estate offers a multitude of advantages for investors. Furthermore, the tangible nature of real estate provides a sense of control and security, while the potential for passive income allows for greater flexibility and freedom. While there are risks associated with real estate investment, they can be mitigated through careful research and wise decision-making. Overall, real estate is a solid investment option for those looking to build long-term wealth and financial security.

Entrepreneurship and Passive Income Generation

In a world steeped in uncertainty, where economic fluctuations and financial downturns seem inevitable, everyone desires stability and security. While there are many paths to financial freedom, the pursuit of entrepreneurship and passive income generation stands out as an exciting and promising avenue for building long-term wealth.

Entrepreneurship, the art of identifying opportunities and transforming them into profitable endeavors, is a key driver of economic growth and personal prosperity. It is a thrilling adventure that allows individuals to control their destiny, unleash their creative potential, and make a lasting impact on the world. By starting their own businesses, entrepreneurs create value, generate jobs, and contribute to the overall prosperity of their communities. Moreover, the long-term wealth created through entrepreneurship extends far beyond financial gains; it encompasses personal growth, self-satisfaction, and a sense of fulfillment.

One of the primary advantages of entrepreneurship is the potential to generate passive income. Passive income refers to earnings that are derived from investments or business activities that require minimal effort or time to maintain. Unlike active income, which necessitates ongoing involvement and effort, passive income streams can continue to generate wealth even when one is not actively working. This aspect of passive income makes it especially attractive for individuals seeking financial stability and freedom.

Passive income can be generated through various means, such as rental properties, dividends from stocks, royalties from creative works, or even online businesses. Real estate investments, for example, offer a reliable and proven method of generating passive income. By purchasing properties and renting them out, individuals can create a consistent stream of income that requires minimal effort once the initial setup is complete. Similarly, investing in dividend-paying stocks allows individuals to earn a share of the company's profits without actively participating in its daily operations.

With the advent of the digital age, the possibilities for generating passive income have expanded exponentially. The internet has ushered in a new era of opportunities, enabling individuals to create and monetize digital products or services. From blogging and affiliate marketing to creating online courses or e-commerce stores, the potentials are vast. Even with a modest investment of time and resources, these ventures can yield significant returns in the long run. Moreover, the scalability and global reach of online businesses provide entrepreneurs with the chance to tap into a worldwide market, further increasing their income potential.

The combination of entrepreneurship and passive income generation offers a powerful approach to building long-term wealth. By starting a business and incorporating passive income streams, individuals can leverage their skills and expertise to create multiple sources of income. This diversification helps mitigate the risks associated with relying on a single income source and provides a cushion against potential economic downturns or industry fluctuations. In essence, it adds layers of stability and resilience to one's financial portfolio.

Building long-term wealth through entrepreneurship and passive income generation requires a proactive and strategic mindset. It involves identifying profitable opportunities, conducting thorough market research, and developing innovative solutions to meet the needs and desires of customers. Building a strong foundation for a business, including effective branding, marketing, and customer service, is essential for long-term success. Likewise, in the realm of passive income generation, careful evaluation of investment opportunities and diligent management of income streams are key to maximizing returns.

While entrepreneurship and the pursuit of passive income offer immense potential, it is important to approach these endeavors with a realistic mindset. Building long-term wealth requires patience, perseverance, and a willingness to learn from failures and setbacks. It may take time for businesses to gain traction and start generating significant profits. Similarly, the returns from passive income streams may not be immediate or substantial initially. However, with dedication, hard work, and a long-term vision, the rewards can be substantial and life-changing.

In addition to the financial benefits, entrepreneurship and passive income generation provide individuals with a sense of freedom and fulfillment. By breaking free from traditional employment and becoming their own boss, entrepreneurs have the flexibility to set their own schedules, pursue their passions, and create a work-life balance tailored to their preferences. Similarly, the ability to generate passive income allows individuals to have more control over their time and enjoy the fruits of their labor without being tied to a traditional 9-to-5 job.

This freedom empowers individuals to live life on their terms and pursue their dreams and aspirations.

Entrepreneurship and passive income generation are not limited to any specific demographic or background. They are accessible to anyone with a vision, determination, and the willingness to take calculated risks. Whether young or old, experienced or novice, anyone can seize the opportunities presented by these avenues to build long-term wealth and create a brighter financial future.

In conclusion, building long-term wealth through entrepreneurship and passive income generation is an exciting and promising path to financial success. By harnessing the power of entrepreneurship, individuals can create businesses that not only generate profits but also make a positive impact on their communities and the world. Additionally, by embracing passive income streams, individuals can create multiple sources of income that provide stability, security, and freedom. While the journey may not always be smooth, with persistence, resilience, and a strategic mindset, the rewards can be both financially and personally fulfilling. So, embrace the opportunities that entrepreneurship and passive income generation offer, and embark on a journey towards building long-term wealth that will empower you to live life on your own terms.

Estate Planning and Wealth Preservation

In a world where financial security and stability are paramount, the quest for long-term wealth becomes a priority for many individuals. While there are numerous avenues to build and accumulate wealth, estate planning and wealth preservation stand out as essential strategies for ensuring financial success and security in the long run.

Estate planning, the meticulous process of managing and distributing assets upon one's death, plays a crucial role in building and preserving long-term wealth. Beyond simply drafting a will, estate planning involves a comprehensive evaluation of one's assets, liabilities, and financial goals. By establishing a clear roadmap for the transfer of assets, beneficiaries can be protected, taxes can be minimized, and the distribution of wealth can be optimized.

One of the primary advantages of estate planning is the ability to mitigate estate taxes. By implementing various strategies, such as establishing trusts, creating gifting strategies, and utilizing tax exemptions, individuals can minimize the tax burden on their estate. This not only ensures that more wealth can be preserved and distributed to loved ones but also safeguards the intergenerational transfer of wealth.

Furthermore, estate planning allows individuals to establish a legacy that reflects their values and aspirations. It provides an opportunity to support charitable causes, create trusts for future generations, and ensure that financial resources are utilized in a manner that aligns with personal beliefs and goals. By carefully considering one's philanthropic desires and incorporating them into estate planning, individuals can leave a lasting impact on their communities and make a difference beyond their lifetime.

Beyond estate planning, wealth preservation strategies are essential for preserving and growing long-term wealth. Wealth preservation refers to the proactive steps taken to safeguard assets from erosion due to various factors, such as inflation, unexpected expenses, or economic downturns. By implementing effective wealth preservation strategies, individuals can protect their capital, maintain their standard of living, and ensure a secure financial future.

Diversification is a fundamental aspect of wealth preservation. By spreading investments across different asset classes, industries, and geographical regions, individuals can minimize the risk associated with market volatility. This ensures that even if one investment underperforms, the overall portfolio remains stable and resilient. Additionally, diversification provides opportunities for growth and capital appreciation, capturing potential returns from different market segments.

Another key aspect of wealth preservation is effective risk management. This involves analyzing potential risks, such as legal liabilities, market fluctuations, or unexpected events, and taking appropriate measures to mitigate them. This may include obtaining insurance coverage, establishing emergency funds, or implementing asset protection strategies. By proactively addressing risks, individuals can protect their wealth from unforeseen circumstances and preserve their financial security.

In addition to diversification and risk management, a long-term outlook is vital in wealth preservation. Successful wealth preservation requires individuals to resist impulsive decisions fueled by short-term market fluctuations or emotional reactions. Instead, having a well-thought-out investment plan and sticking to it, even during turbulent times, can yield favorable long-term results. Patience, discipline, and a focus on the big picture are key.

Moreover, seeking professional guidance and expertise in wealth preservation is crucial. Working with financial advisors, estate planning attorneys, and tax professionals can provide individuals with the necessary knowledge and strategies to preserve and grow their wealth effectively. These professionals can help navigate complex legal and financial landscapes, offering personalized solutions tailored to individual circumstances and goals.

While building long-term wealth through estate planning and wealth preservation requires careful planning and implementation, the benefits are significant. By taking a proactive approach to managing assets and protecting them from erosion, individuals can build a solid foundation for financial success and security. It allows individuals to ensure their loved ones are financially supported, charitable causes are promoted, and personal aspirations are fulfilled.

Furthermore, estate planning and wealth preservation provide individuals with peace of mind and a sense of control over their financial future. The knowledge that one's wealth is protected, growing, and being utilized in alignment with personal values allows for a greater sense of financial security and confidence. It enables individuals to focus on other aspects of their lives, knowing that their wealth is being managed responsibly and with a long-term perspective.

Building long-term wealth through estate planning and wealth preservation is a prudent and optimistic approach to financial security and success. By carefully planning for the distribution of assets, minimizing tax burdens, and establishing a legacy, individuals can ensure that their wealth is preserved and utilized in accordance with their wishes. Incorporating diverse and resilient investment strategies, implementing risk management measures, and seeking professional guidance further enhance wealth preservation efforts. Ultimately, estate planning and wealth preservation provide the foundation for a secure and prosperous financial future, allowing individuals to enjoy the fruits of their labor and leave a lasting legacy.

Acknowledgements

I am immensely grateful to my parents for their unwavering support and guidance throughout my life's journey. In particular, I want to acknowledge and express my deepest appreciation to my father, who has had a profound impact on shaping the person I have blossomed into.

Since a young age, my dad instilled in me a sense of purpose and ambition, planting seeds of wisdom and insight that have guided me in pursuing my desires and plans. His heartfelt encouragement and belief in my abilities have been a constant source of motivation, empowering me to overcome challenges and pursue my dreams with unwavering determination.

My dad's presence and influence have been a steady pillar of strength, providing not only practical advice but also emotional support during times of uncertainty. He taught me the importance of perseverance, integrity, and resilience, qualities that have served as the foundation of my growth.

His belief in my potential has fueled my ambition, enabling me to push beyond my comfort zone and embrace new opportunities. Through his own actions and achievements, my dad has exemplified the power of passion and dedication, inspiring me to strive for excellence in everything I put my hands to and plant my feet toward.

I am forever grateful to my father for his unwavering love, guidance, and the invaluable insights he has instilled in me. My achievements and successes are a testament to his profound influence, and I was blessed to have him as my dad.

www.ingramcontent.com/pod-product-compliance
Lightning Source LLC
Chambersburg PA
CBHW070029110426
42741CB00034B/2694